Books are to be returned on or before
the last date below.

SR

Titles in the FULL FLIGHT ✈ runway » series

Badger Publishing Limited
Suite G08, Business & Technology Centre
Bessemer Drive, Stevenage, Hertfordshire, SG1 2DX
Telephone: 01438 791037   Fax: 01438 791036
www.badger-publishing.co.uk

A Big Catch ISBN 978 1 84691 844 5

Publisher: David Jamieson
Editor: Danny Pearson
Design: Fiona Grant
Illustration: Aleksander Sotirovski

CONTENTS

Badger Publishing

Vocabulary:

Fair

Biggest

Caught/Catch

Shouted

Photo

Quick

Main characters:

Zach

Connor

CHAPTER 1
BACK IN TOWN

One Saturday, the fair came to town.

Zach was happy. His friend, Connor, was with the fair.

On Sunday, Zach and Connor went fishing.

CHAPTER 2
A BIG CATCH

Zach caught two little fish.

But Connor caught one very big fish.

"Quick Zach! You must take a photo of this!" shouted Connor. "It must be the biggest catch of my life!"

9

But just then, a little girl fell in the river so Zach didn't take the photo.

"Quick!" Zach shouted to
the girl,
"Grab this!"
But it was no good.

CHAPTER 3
HELP!

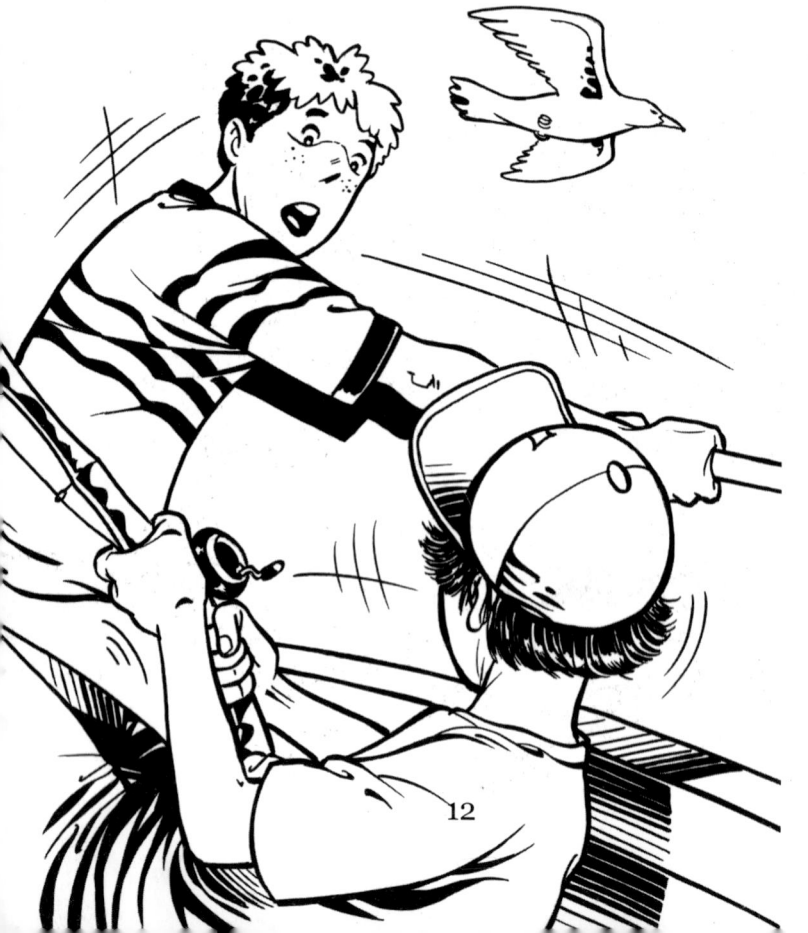

"Quick, Connor!" shouted Zach.

"You must help the little girl."

Connor helped the girl.

Zach took a photo.

The little girl was very happy.

Her Mum and Dad were very happy, too.

But Connor wasn't happy.

He had lost the biggest catch of his life!

But on Friday,

Zach showed Connor the paper.

"There's a photo of you in here!"

he said.

A BIG CATCH!

Questions:

What day did the fair come to Zach's town?

What would you take if you went fishing?

How many fish did Zach catch?

Who took the photo of the rescue?

Where did the photo of the rescue end up?

Missing

by Alison Hawes

illustrated by
Aleksander Sotirovski

Contents

Vocabulary:

Earthquake   China

Watching/Watch   Appeal

Cousins   Reply

Main characters:

An

Li

Mum

Dad

Chapter 1
Earthquake!

An and Li are watching television.

There is an earthquake in China.

"Quick, Mum, Dad!" says An.

"Come and see this!"

Mum and Dad are crying.

"This is where your cousins live!" they say.

Dad and Mum phone their cousins.

They try for days and days.

But there is no reply.

Chapter 2
No Reply

An and Li email their cousins.

They try for days and days.

But there is no reply.

An and Li sell cakes at school.

They give the money to the earthquake appeal.

Mum and Dad walk for miles and miles.
They give the money to the earthquake
appeal.

Months and months go by.

But still there is no reply.

Chapter 3
The Search

Dad says, "I am going to find our cousins."

Days and days go by.

But at last Dad gets to the town.

Dad looks and looks.

At last, he finds his cousins' house.

But there is nothing left.

A man sees Dad crying

"Don't cry," he says. "Your cousins are living at my house!"

Dad runs and runs.

He doesn't stop until he sees his cousins!

Questions:

Where did the Earthquake happen?

How did Mum and Dad try to find out if their cousins were OK?

How did An and Li try to find out if their cousins were OK?

How did Dad get to China ?

Are the family's cousins OK?

Where are they staying?